A GUIDE TO MENTAL HEALTH AT WORK

How to help colleagues cope with stress and depression

By Sir John Timpson

Published in 2019 by Timpson Limited.

All rights are reserved. No reproduction, copy or transmission of this publication, whether in whole or in part, may be made without prior consent of the publisher.

Timpson House, Claverton Road, Wythenshawe, Manchester M23 9TT .
Tel: 0161 946 6200 www.timpson.com

ISBN: 978-0-9576613-8-7

Design and illustration.co.uk)

D1341113

This is a book for everyone. We can all improve mental health at work but most of us need to know more about the subject.

This guide describes the symptoms, suggests ways that people with stress and depression can help themselves and gives hints on how leaders and colleagues can make a difference.

Stress and depression can hit anyone.

But the busiest and most conscientious
people can be at the greatest risk.

Most thrive

Some struggle

A few are unwell

We all have mental health and it can fluctuate between thriving, struggling and feeling unwell.

If all of us are more aware of our own and other people's mental health much can be done to improve well-being at work.

There is a limit to how much work
anyone can do, but some people
still force themselves to do even more!

Some people take on too much - both at work and at home. Eventually they hit a crucial moment when they start staring into space.

For a time people can put on a face
and no one notices how they
really feel.

Everyone can wake up
feeling a bit down...

...we all have good days
and bad days...

...but this is different.

Lots of people carry on for fear of having a mental health problem, letting others down, being considered a failure, losing their job and never working again.

Many of those with stress feel they are surrounded by happy people who can all cope with life without a care in the world.

They reckon everyone is talking behind their back.

But without knowing they are ill why should anyone else make allowances?

The first step on the road to recovery is to pluck up the courage to tell someone things aren't okay.

ADVICE TO ANYONE STRUGGLING

You need help - trying to cope on your own will only make you feel worse. The sooner you get help the sooner your life will get back on track. Telling someone you have a problem doesn't make you less of a person.

Don't be ashamed, be proud that you are facing up to reality.

4 TIPS ON HOW TO GET HELP

1. Talk to a friend.

Pick the person who is easiest to talk to

2. (If you feel you can) Talk to your boss.

3. Find out about the help avaiable.

4. Go to the doctor.

I think I need help.

The longer you wait the worse things can get.

It makes a big difference if your boss is someone you can talk to.

But even with a sympathetic boss it is difficult to start the conversation.

STARTING A CONVERSATION

The first words are the most difficult but these could help...

I've been meaning to talk to you for some time.

I'm hoping that you can help me.

I'm worried about letting down the rest of the team.

I haven't been well for a few weeks.

I know I haven't been on top form.

It doesn't really matter what you say - what matters is that you are talking about it.

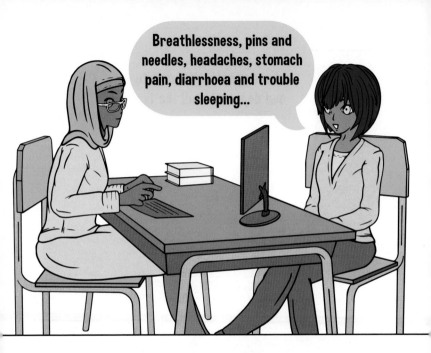

Due to shame and guilt many start talking about physical symptoms and only mention anxiety/depression as they are about to leave the surgery.

Many people with stress and depression think they are the only ones in the world to suffer - **NOT TRUE** - at least one person in four experiences the same symptoms.

COMMON SYMPTOMS

Lack of self esteem

Loss of appetite or comfort eating

Poor memory, no concentration

Lack of sex drive

Wanting to be alone - not wishing to meet anyone.

Worse in the morning better as the day goes on.

Flu   Depression   Broken leg

It's a physical problem (your doctor will explain)
just like flu or a broken leg.

But others can't see any signs of your illness.

Head
Teacher

Olympic
Champion

Chief
Executive

Senior
Nurse

Top jobs can be the most stressful.

People in senior roles are more likely
to suffer from stress and depression
because they tend to push
themselves to breaking point.

But people don't have to be in a high
profile job to experience problems.

Issac Newton

Sigmund Freud

Ernest Hemmingway

Abraham Lincoln

Agatha Christie

John Lennon

Tony Hancock

Marilyn Monroe

Winston Churchill

Charles Dickens

John D. Rockefeller

Beethoven

Lots of well-known high achievers
suffered from stress and depression.

LOOK AFTER YOURSELF

Some people simply don't know when to stop - they can't say no, always wanting to do better, please other people and finish every job.

Consequently they are so hard on themselves they go a step too far and reach breaking point - but they still won't give up - making matters even worse.

Counsellors can help patients to understand much more about their illness so they can help themselves get back to being at their best. They may mention that sleep, diet, exercise and mindfulness can all play a part in preventing high levels of stress.

TYPICAL TRIGGER POINTS AT WORK

Statement of fitness for work
For social security or Statutory Sick Pay

Patient's name	(Mr,) Mrs, Miss, Ms S. O. Lowe
I assessed your case on:	4 / 1 / 2019
and, because of the following condition(s):	Stress and depression

I advise you that:

[X] you are not fit for work.

[ ] you may be fit for work taking account of the following advice:

If available, and with your employer's agreement, you may benefit from:

[ ] a phased return to work   [ ] amended duties

[ ] altered hours   [ ] workplace adaptations

Comments, including functional effects of your condition(s):

Give your brain a break. Take at least two weeks off and don't look at any work for more than 10 minutes at a time. Relax watching daytime television.

This will be the case for   2 weeks

or from   4 / 1 / 2019   to   18 / 1 / 2019

I will/will not need to assess your fitness for work again at the end of this period.
(Please delete as applicable)

Doctor's signature

Date of statement   4 / 1 / 2019

Doctor's address

Doctor's medical practice
23 The Road
Manchester
M44 44YY

Med3 04/10

SICK LEAVE

Time for some convalescence.

It is difficult for others to understand what
stress and depression are like.

Even well meaning advice
can be unhelpful.

My mother got better by joining a choir and making new friends.

Why don't you get out to The Comedy Club and have a good laugh - it is bound to make you feel better!

I know someone with depression who got a dog - it made a massive difference.

Bosses have a key role to play - but
standard management practice
may be inappropriate.

HOW A BOSS...

I have to send you a warning letter!

You are letting the team down!

I'm giving you an easier job!

...CAN MAKE THINGS WORSE

You are being put on a performance management programme!

We've been very patient. It is time you made a real effort to snap yourself out of it!

I'll give you three months to sort yourself out!

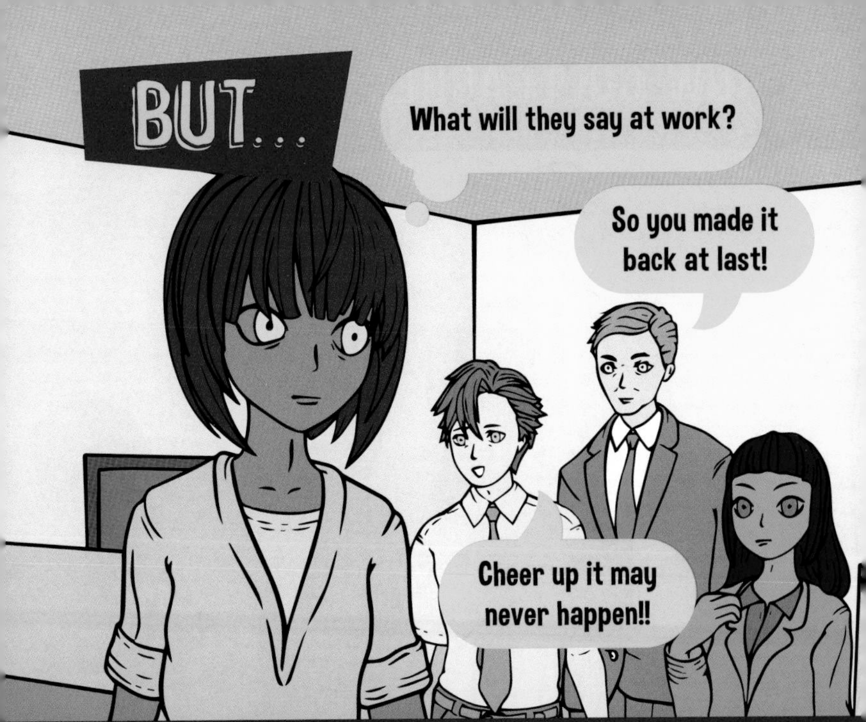

"I'm worried about going back to work."

HOW COLLEAGUES CAN HELP

If colleagues at work learn enough about stress and depression they can be really helpful. They realise that a valuable colleague has recovered from an illness and with their support get back to being the best they can be.

Make sure every colleague feels part of
the team - being included helps them
feel safe and will build confidence.

GREAT BOSS

A boss can make a major difference to
colleagues with mental health problems.

WHAT A BOSS CAN DO TO HELP

Come and see me straight away.

BE AVAILABLE

I've got as long as you like.

BE PATIENT

It can't be easy for you.

BE UNDERSTANDING

I'm here to help however I can.

BE KIND

I think you should go and see the doctor.

BE HELPFUL

Take the next week off and then give me a ring for a chat.

BE FLEXIBLE

A boss can do a lot to help a colleague get back into the work place after a spell away.

HELPFUL ADVICE

Take it steady.

Don't rush into anything.

Tell me if you need to take time off.

Pop in anytime if you have a problem.

FLEXIBLE WORKING

Whenever possible, let colleagues fit
their work around the rest of their lives.

For someone recovering from stress
and depression the ability to take a
break can make all the difference.

How to be a great boss

A boss can have a massive influence
on the mental health of their team.

A great boss doesn't simply sit in the office, give orders and chair meetings.

Your colleagues run the business, so get to know them as well as you can.

That means meeting face-to-face - you can't spot a great personality by studying personnel records on a computer.

Managers are in a privileged position - they can influence more people than clergy, doctors, social workers, teachers and politicians.

A big part of the role is being a mentor - helping to solve the problems that fill a colleague's mind with worry.

TIP

Keep in touch with colleagues who are off work and offer a home visit

DO YOU KNOW YOUR PEOPLE?

DO YOU KNOW YOUR PEOPLE?

SUBJECT... (put randomly selected name here)

All the questions relate to your chosen subject

	Points Available
PARTNERS NAME	10
LAST HOLIDAY	10
PETS	10
HOBBIES	5
WHAT HE/SHE WOULD LIKE FOR BIRTHDAY (£20)	5
WHAT DOES HE/SHE DRINK	5
WHAT CAR	5
FOOTBALL TEAM	5
CHILDREN – NAMES AND AGES	20
WHERE IS HOME	
FAVOURITE TELEVISION PROGRAM	5
TASTE IN MUSIC (eg. Rock. Pop. Jazz. Classical)	10
IDEA OF A NIGHT OUT (eg. Night Club. Cinema. Restaurant. Pub)	5
	5

MORE THAN 70 → You are a people person

LESS THAN 70 → Get to know your staff before taking the test again

96

Understanding a colleague means knowing their interests when they are away from the organisation.

Most of your colleagues' worries have little
to do with work - feel privileged to help.

ORDINARY BOSS

POLICIES
DEPARTMENTAL MEETINGS
APPRAISALS
KPI'S
QUARTERLY REPORTS
GUIDELINES

GREAT BOSS

KINDNESS
PERSONAL MENTOR
TRAINING
"THANK YOU"
"WELL DONE"
SPECIAL REWARDS
BIRTHDAY OFF

AMAZE YOUR COLLEAGUES

A great boss looks after the team
and helps every colleague become
the best they can possibly be.

The way an organisation is managed
has a big influence on the colleagues'
health and well-being.

IMPORTANCE OF FEELING VALUED

Early years

Family

And at work

Neighbours

Friends

Our personal confidence and self-esteem is developed by the attachment we form with others.

This starts in childhood and goes on to include life at work.

Every work place should create a
happy community - giving a safe base
to colleagues who look forward to
coming to work.

An organisation dominated by red tape and process can cause dedicated and talented colleagues to feel overworked and under valued.

Star performers work extra hard to compensate for a rigid regime but may become so stressed they move elsewhere. Leaving the organisation to be run by people who care more about themselves and less about the business. No wonder rigidly run organisations can be so inefficient.

Trust your colleagues with the freedom to
do their job in the way they know best.

GREAT PEOPLE
MAKE A GREAT BUSINESS

MR HELPFUL

MRS HAPPY

MR KEEN

MR FRIENDLY

MISS SKILLFUL

MR PUNCTUAL

MR QUICK

MR PERSONALITY

MR AMBITIOUS

MR FUN TO BE WITH

MRS HONEST

MR CAN'T STOP SMILING

Pick people with a positive personality
who will be respected by their
colleagues.

IF A COLLEAGUE HAS PICKED THE WRONG JOB

MR SCRUFFY

MS LATE

MR IS IT FIVE 'O' CLOCK

MR RUDE

MR CARELESS

MISS DON'T CARE

MR GRUMPY

MR DULL

MRS SLOW

MR SCROUNGER

MR DISHONEST

MISS FIB

HELP THEM FIND THEIR HAPPINESS ELSEWHERE
GENEROUSLY/NICELY/QUICKLY

Make sure your great colleagues work alongside people who love coming to work as much as they do.

Support for colleagues with stress and depression isn't simply provided by a process or through appointing a mental health officer.

An organisation's culture makes the real difference.

MENTAL HEALTH FIRST AIDERS

How can I help?

INSTANT COUNSELLING

Ideally every organisation should provide easy access to a qualified counsellor and train a number of key colleagues to be mentors, with the skills to talk about mental health.

GREAT PLACE TO WORK

The best answers are found in a happy
workplace based on kindness and respect
where everyone understands the
background to stress and depression.

THE GOOD NEWS

Nearly everyone returns to top form

For anyone in the depths of despair
it is reassuring to know that one
day almost everyone will feel
much better.

The sign of a great workplace.

HELPFUL WEBSITES

www.mind.org.uk
www.mentalhealthatwork.org.uk
www.mindfulemployer.net
affinityhealthhub.co.uk
www.bitc.org.uk